Candy From Strangers
poetry by kellie elmore

This publication is a work of fiction. Names, characters, places, and incidents either are products of the author's imagination or are used fictitiously. This work is protected in full by all applicable copyright laws, as well as by misappropriation, trade secret, unfair competition, and other applicable laws. No part of this book may be reproduced or transmitted in any manner without written permission from Winter Goose Publishing, except in the case of brief quotations embodied in critical articles or reviews. All rights reserved.

Winter Goose Publishing
2701 Del Paso Road, 130-92
Sacramento, CA 95835

www.wintergoosepublishing.com
Contact Information: info@wintergoosepublishing.com

Candy From Strangers

COPYRIGHT © 2013 by Kellie Elmore

First Edition, December 2013

Paperback ISBN: 978-1-941058-02-2

Cover Art by Winter Goose Publishing
Typeset by Odyssey Books

Published in the United States of America

Six years ago, when I began sharing my writing online, I didn't realize the amazing world that would open up to me. This almost secret society of poets and writers, that are so passionate about the written word, revealed itself to me and allowed me a place inside its bubble. This collection is for all of those who encourage me every day. For those who inspire me to step outside my comfort zone and not be afraid of being different. I consider them family and thank each of them for holding my hand as I travel different paths on this journey. This one is for those who gave me courage to think outside the box. I hope you enjoy what came of it.

Wise Words from a Drunken Ghost

It was already noon and I had been up all night fighting with my head, trying to spit out anything I could with a paralyzed tongue and a numb hand. The same old man who had been eyeballing me all day, sat there chain-smoking, under the sound of cracking pool balls, watching me with a shit-eating smirk as I erased a hole through my paper, again and again. Then, he clutched a nearly empty bottle of dark liquor and hobbled over. He leaned in to me and said . . .

You're trying too hard, honey. Bar tales will tell themselves. What you're looking for is out there. There are no stories in this dive, just cheating wives and backslid preachers, unless you put them together, which I assume they already are. You gotta go dig in all the other dirty holes of the world. You can find some good shit in the faces of strangers . . . the kind of shit you can't make up. Just watch them, and soon, they'll tell you their stories. It'll be like taking candy . . .

And everybody has one; your job is to take the goddam boring out of it.

But you gotta go. You've got to leave these cockroaches behind and get the hell outa here. Drive, take a bus, or throw up your thumb, whatever gets you gone.

He raised his glass to the bartender, nodding for another round.

Or you could stay, and take up drinking, but that won't get you anywhere, it might get you in the smut paper, but it sure as hell won't get you out of my booth.

I quickly scooped up my notebook and slid out of my seat and as I opened the door, letting in the light that wrapped around the smoke, I turned back and asked his name. He held up his drink and said . . .

You can call me Hank, baby.

Contents

Wise Words from a Drunken Ghost	v

Part One — 1
Bar Tales	1
Cigarettes and Lipstick Napkins	3
The Widow	4
On the Rocks	5
A Girl Named Allyce	6
Dive	7
A Cowboy and a Stripper	8
Miss Kitty	9
He Was a Changed Man	10
Happy Pills	11
Blue Collar Man	12
Three's a Crowd	13
That Whore Delilah	14
To Be a Shoe	15
Her Name was Angel	17
Kisses from Karma	18
Women	19

Part Two — 21
Pumping Gas	23
He Stopped for a Drag on the Sidewalk	25
Lovers	26
Pennies and Spam	27
Holy Shit	28

Stranger in the SUV	30
On My Way to Georgia	31
Marilyn's Cigarette	33
Slow Ride	34
A Spoon Full of Guilt	35
The Sad Girl in the Window	36
Good Old Fashioned Liars	37
First Offense Inmate	38
Moonshiners	39
Spandex and Drooling Dogs	40
Thrift Store Surprise	41
Reality Check	42
An Old Man in the Park	43
Suburbia	44
The Empty House Next Door	46
The Tin Man in a Pretty Yard	47
Talk Radio	48
John Brown	50
The Lights Never Go Out	52
Whiskey and Vinyl	53
The Witness	54
Fucking Telemarketers	55
Small Town Politician	56
The Pneumonia	57
Early Risers	59
The Girl at Register Three	62
Finding Jesus at the Discount Grocery	63
Truck Stop Bathroom	65
About the Author	67

Part One
Bar Tales

Cigarettes and Lipstick Napkins

Cheap perfume trails behind
as she stumbles through smoke
and fondling hands
in two-inch drunken heels
that flatter her still
nicely firm bare calves.
The bass vibrates her chest
and vodka warms her face,
rouging her high cheekbones
to match the crumpled napkins
and glass rims on the bar,
kissed by ruby colored lipstick.

Aged bedroom eyes peer
through a glaze of smudged mascara,
and a blurred wave
of three hundred drunks.

Head spinning,
she meets the dance floor
and in an *almost* provocative,
staggered sway,
she seductively massages
the smooth fabric
of her low-cut, thrift store
scarlet dress.
Twisting long ashen locks
around tingling fingers,
now baring two less rings,
and for the first time in twenty years,
she feels *sexy.*

The Widow

She didn't want to tell him of the last one who owned her heart
the one who she thought would sit by her on the swing
watching each-other's hair turn silver and
faces form wrinkles in the corners of their mouths
from the many years of laughter they would share.
She didn't want to tell him that he was dead,
that she was left to swing alone on the porch of
the house they bought on their second anniversary,
on the same porch where now, someone new
was asking for her company at dinner,
because then he may pity her.
The widow.
And should he find that she is boring,
or that she eats too slowly and they will always
be late for the movie,
he may be reluctant enough to just
say goodnight and never call back,
all because he feels sorry for her,
because he would know that when she goes in
and the lights turn off
she will crawl into his side of the bed
and cry herself to sleep,
and what kind of man does that to a woman
who lost her husband
ten years ago?

On the Rocks

gaunt
and unshaven,
the whiskey; chestnut
only reminded him of her eyes
and he would drown again
on that barstool on the end

A Girl Named Allyce

she waltzed in lookin' like a cheap bar maid
all dolled up in Grandma's lace
a little extra on the backside
nicely proportioned to
even out the beauts on her front-side
wherever she went,
things would get real hard, real quick
not much favored with the ladies
noses north due to her buxom bosom
unable to contain in such snug velour
and boys stuttering
Allyce, may I buy you a drink
whispers, leers, and *how dare she*
and not because they were jealous
no, of course not.
Allyce sure had a way about her
planting jaws on the floor
and hands around spitting shafts
while they closed their eyes
and imagined she said yes

Dive

He stole her lips with a hungered stare
in his blatant attempt at seduction
though barely rousing her interest
he assumed his callous swagger
would leave her zealously begging
for a lewd go-round in the men's room
reeking of piss and sweaty ass
clearly mistaking bawdiness with chivalry
confident he would get off
dipping himself inside her mouth
or even,
if he plays his benevolence card
as a last resort, certainly
her panties would magically drop
convulsing spasms of laughter
she attempted to hold inside
and then, she spewed
soiling the crotch of his Wranglers
in a mouthful of Budweiser
thwarting his contemptible efforts
with sheer revel

A Cowboy and a Stripper

I watched him watching her
leaning over the rail
alongside the stage
with a bottle of beer in his hand
and a big, gold belt buckle
with the name Buck on it

she moved, sultry and tempting
dipping and rolling her hips
and he was taken in
I could tell by the way his mouth
began to slightly part and
his eyes peeked from the darkness of
the shadow cast from his cowboy hat

and I began to understand why
they relate men to dogs
as he stood there heated

I sipped my whiskey sour
and stole cherries from the garnish tray
my cheeks burning with jealousy
wanting his eyes on me
wanting any eyes on me, but
I wasn't willing to take off my clothes
for a buck

Miss Kitty

Miss Kitty was a lover
honey, baby, sugar buns
free hugs to anyone,
especially the boys.
When she walked into a room,
her hips followed her lips
and she'd lick her finger
nice and slow
and point to who she wanted
to take home.
Eager little fellas
worked up over her
dominant presence, ready
and willing to be her toy,
but in dark corners
when the time came
they found Miss Kitty
was a boy.

He Was a Changed Man

He talked about God and the way things should be
as he cracked open another bottle of beer
on his forearm with a tattoo of a naked
dancing hula girl without a skirt.
I'm a changed man. Jail will do that to ya,
he said with a sour look on his face after
taking a big swallow of his Miller draft,
holding the bottle out in front of him
turning it to inspect the date on the side.
This goddamn shit is green!
Can't a man get a decent bottle of beer
in this fucking place?
he shouted as he smashed it at his feet.
As I was saying . . . he said.

Happy Pills

She chased her dreams down
crushing pain into powder
when she lost herself to
the grit of the city
and the fast lane spun her out.
Everyone had told her *no,*
except for the men underneath her
screaming *yes, yes, yes.*
She came as a kid,
a long way from Kansas,
but still wound up blown away,
caught up in a back-alley rush,
somewhere off Broadway.

Blue Collar Man

he served twenty-eight years
for her smile and five acres
of the American dream
grindin' out metal
factory work without a title
watching white collars fake interest
as he tried explaining
just what it was he did
laughing inside
because he knew they saw him
as a walking country song
and he thought to himself
you just can't teach appreciation

Three's a Crowd

He said *beautiful* with a period
as if she was just to believe it's true.
His definition,
so shallow and spoken with egotistical boast
in his love-drunk gaze.
She laughs
as he attempts once more to persuade her,
stealing her Marlboro from between her fingers,
pressing it out in the ashtray.
I can't help but wonder if he knows what I'm thinking:
"Loser."
Tickling my humor,
amused only by his silly word games and
how he thinks the tequila is doing the trick,
and I blow my smoke in his face.
She whispers to me.
I almost want to kiss him,
but only to taint his mouth with my cigarette breath
and watch him pretend not to notice.

And she leans in closely,
Sure, I'll have another drink.
So I'm beautiful, you say?

That Whore Delilah

she held the words
between clenched fingers
on trembling hands
as they tugged at her gut
like balloons in the wind
deflating disillusions in
sobbing echoes
pressed between the pages
of Polaroid memories
she'd found his manifest of
capricious reasons and
perfumed *need-you-now*s
it was Delilah after all
tucked secretly away inside
a shoebox past
both of them lying now
in crumbled wads on the floor

To Be a Shoe

In the rearview mirror,
I watched as he
gripped her arm
just above the elbow
and tugged at her
all the way to the
car parked beside me
from the tavern entrance.
His flannel shirt
unbuttoned, showing his
round, hairy beer gut
that hung low over top
his ripped jeans.
And her pale, round,
pregnant belly wrapped in
a dingy wife-beater
that sat atop her small frame.
She waddled quickly across the
hot pavement in flip-flops
that smacked against her heels.
He shoved her down in the seat
and slammed the door
nearly catching her foot, and
her shoe fell to the ground.
You dumb bitch.
Don't ever come looking for me again,
he shouted as he backed up
and squealed tires.
And she stared longingly
at her shoe, still lying there

as they pulled out.
And I bet she wanted to
be that shoe.

Her Name was Angel

She sat on the hood of a sixty-nine Camaro,
belonging to one of the hot-blooded boys
gathered around her, holding their cans of
cheap beer, fighting for her attention.
She teased them with nonchalant touches
of her hand on their arm and tossed her
straight, thin hair away from her face,
throwing her head back, laughing out loud
just to be laughing because, one of those
boys told her it was cute. *I'm so hot*,
she said as she started to pull off her
short, denim jacket and they jumped to
help her pull her arms from the sleeves.
And spread across her back was a tattoo of
wings. Her name was Angel and those
were the only wings she'll ever see.

Kisses from Karma

He stands there popping his knuckles,
grimacing,
as the opposition lie on the ground,
blood pulsating from his nostrils,
muttering through a split tongue
and missing teeth.
The crowd, on their feet
roaring affirmation.
He raises his fist,
kisses karma on the lips
and thanks her for a sweeter kiss
than the one old split lip stole from his girl.

Women

she pranced out the door
a half lit hot mess
high-stepping in platform heels
twisting her hips
and tossing her hair
like she was famous

she looked around her
back and forth like
she wanted to catch someone
watching her
and I was

and I shook my head
thinking
who she thought
she must be as I,
behind my tinted glass,
pulled my shades from my head
and drove away
like I was famous

Part Two

Strangers in Passing

Pumping Gas

I am no better than you
and you are no better than him
we are all standing here
pumping gas and daydreaming

I looked around
at blank-faced travelers
heading to different destinations
going in different directions
trying to make a dollar and
spending their dollars, in both
fancy cars and beat up clunkers

The highway is just another
Line in our story
And the road doesn't care
What we're driving
As we travel through
Like the story doesn't care
If we're in our pajamas
While we read it
All that matters is
Whether or not we enjoyed
The ride it took us on
Because there's always an end
Some will find it
Sputtering on fumes
And some will be stopped
With a full tank and
An engine at full throttle

But we all end up in front
Of that same dead-end sign
When the gas runs out

He Stopped for a Drag on the Sidewalk

funny, the ideas that entertain
some people, he thought
I laugh inside
when I think of how they perceive
this world, as theirs
and people
other people
as lesser, invaluable
staring at me over their newspaper
my beer in hand
and smoke hanging from my lip
hey
you shit the same as I do, buddy
what they think
but won't say
I'm not supposed to be here
in their little bubble
of ass kissing
and punching clocks
behind mahogany desks
stripped from my woods
that I pitch my tent beneath
fucking thieves
stealing my air
out of my goddamn bubble

Lovers

She hit him with those baby blues
like a sucker-punch to the gut,
bringing him to his knees.
He never stands a chance against them;
he's putty every time.

She didn't care
that she had to be the one to ask.
He wanted to, but always chickened out.
It didn't matter though,
'cause she wore the pants anyway.

Vegas bound with pawn-shop bands,
and parched skin from desert winds
stuck to cracked leather seats
with a prime view of a real western sunset,
all from the front seat of his two-grand convertible.

And they said we'd never go anywhere, baby.

Pennies and Spam

She slipped a can of Spam in the pocket
of her long, wool coat that hung below
her denim shorts and just above a pair of
army boots with a floppy heal on the left
that looked like it had come loose and
unglued at the sole, just like her.
She walked over to the window that faced
the parking lot of the convenience store
and pointed her finger in a stabbing motion
at a carload of kids sitting in a
beat-up station wagon with brown paneling.
They sat back in the seats, appearing fearful
of an impending ass whooping if they didn't
shut up and sit down as I assumed her
stabbing finger implied to them.
She reached the register with a sleeve of
saltine crackers and a handful of
sticky, corroded pennies like the kind
you find in the cup-holder of your car
after a paper cup leaks onto them.
All pennies and her total was a dollar
and ninety-nine cents.
I threw twenty bucks on the counter and
told her to keep the change—
a little glue for her soul.

Holy Shit

Jesus Saves was painted boldly on the
back of an old, brown station-wagon,
a lead footed driver behind the wheel.
Steady cruising the long, straight highway
ahead of her when
he tosses a lottery scratch-off ticket
out of his window and it sticks
to her windshield.
Son of a—
She reaches her hand out to pull it off,
then tosses it into her console.

An old man exits the gas station,
his fingers digging in a deli bag,
pulling out fried chicken livers and
popping them into his jaw, chewing like
he didn't have one tooth in his head.
She thought, *I'm starving and still
seven hundred and eighty-two miles to go,*
when the payphone on the corner of the lot yells,
Call home!

*God help me before I even let them think
they were right. No, I'd rather be stuck here in . . .
where am I? This piss-hole town between
Fort Damned and Mount Shit!*

She takes one more long, hard drag before tossing her
last sanity stick into the wind and crawls back

into her beater Bonneville with the sun-cracked dash
and scorching pleather seat that burns her ass.
She grabs the lottery ticket from the cup-holder
to make room for her can of Pepsi when she notices
the numbers match and the prize is five hundred dollars.

Holy Shit!

Stranger in the SUV

The road does not belong to you,
this is not highway "get the fuck over"
or interstate "for the richer than you,"
and I see you on your cellphone—*pretending*.
Bullying me from the driver seat,

yet too goddamn scared to look at me when you pass.
I see you laughing,
while you blow by me
burning money out your ass in an invisible plume
of smoke that's killing us all, even the flowers
in the median are ducking for cover,
that's how they appear anyway.
And while you are looking at me through the rearview,
or checking your lipstick,
I'm looking at the trooper ahead,
also ducked in the median.
Ah, and there's good old karma
as he lights 'em up,
and you tap your brakes—
too late now,
he's got you.

Do you see me laughing?

On My Way to Georgia

He had his thumb stuck out
stepping backward along the
side of the highway,
gripping the satchel
dangling off his left shoulder.
I drove on by.
A mile or so up the road
I turned around.

Where ya headed?
Anywhere south.
You got a gun?
No.
A knife?
No.
Liquor?
Yeah.
Get in.

We pulled off at a bar in Georgia.
Bought a dime off a big redneck
propped up against his Chevy
in the gravel parking lot.
We rolled two,
smoked one,
and he caught a ride out
with a brunette named Debbie.
In trade for the other joint.
He thanked me with his flask.
On the side there was an engraving

that read "keep this full
and you'll never be empty again."
I twisted open the lid and
that's all I remember.

Marilyn's Cigarette

It was on an old dirt road
and I slowed down when I saw her there.
She couldn't have been more than twelve,
just a skinny little girl with dirty
dishwater blond hair, standing beside the road
with a cigarette in her hand.
I guess she thought it made her look grown
and *cool* to the other girls circled around her
and she held it like Marilyn Monroe,
one arm wrapped around her waist and the other
propped up on her side with it loosely hanging
between her two dirty little fingers.
I slowed to a stop and rolled my window down.
She rolled her eyes at me like she was
expecting me to say something motherly,
but all I wanted was one of her smokes.

Slow Ride

Hippies—
free love, peace, and more
free love
giving it
taking it
showing it
bare breasts jiggling
out of the side of their
psychedelic painted van
she was wearing
mirrored sunglasses
and a scarf in her hair
jiggling boobs and
a blowing scarf
eight miles an hour
down the highway
slow ride—
I think they were stoned.

A Spoon Full of Guilt

morning stirred with secrecy
at the cafe downtown
as she sipped on memories
eyes drowning in creamy swirls
sinking her spoon into last night
as he read headlines
that would never tell him
what she had done
while he too dipped his spoon
into guilty recollections
of the girl who brings him coffee

The Sad Girl in the Window

shelves stocked with fairy-tales
in a room strung with white lights
where she wished on them like stars
and painted the ceiling with dreams
waiting to be rescued, waiting to be
a girl they would write stories about
the nobody girl who wins the prince, but
for now she could only pretend, running
away to fields with blue skies that
called to her from a world that lie inside
a glittered snow globe on the bookshelf
whispering that happy
really does exist somewhere
and she wears her best dress, sipping mocha
just in case ever-after decides to
show up on his white horse and
shatter her glass house of dreams

Good Old Fashioned Liars

He came trotting down the courthouse steps,
a big-bellied lawyer with a stink that would
turn a pig's stomach, chuckling and tugging at
his belt, as if to loosen it from around his
wide waistline and he looked miserable;
fat man in a suit and tie, sweating and
wheezing, hobbling his way across the street.
And he entered the restaurant to glutton himself
on a fried chicken and cornbread buffet in
the Americana themed diner on the corner,
a testament to old fashioned values, yet
sitting full of crooked suits who lie for a living.

First Offense Inmate

They were headed for lock-up,
a prison bus loaded with
young men who fucked up,
leaving the fenced back lot
of the county jail.
It pulled out slowly and
every head was face-forward,
blank and mindful of
what lie ahead for them,
except one.
He stared out the window
taking in the streets and
his mother,
who never looked up,
and he turned his head,
watching intently,
with a plea in his eyes,
forgive me.

Moonshiners

His truck was backed up
To the deck door at the co-op
Loading up with bags of corn feed
And whispers of copper and mash
Slipped secrets from his
Tobacco stained lips
As he rolled a toothpick
From side to side
Runnin' at two a.m., he said
Fifty jugs
He wasn't talking about taters

Spandex and Drooling Dogs

His head was hanging out the window,
tongue out, a smile in his eyes,
drooling and licking his lips,
watching women walk by the car
in tight, spandex workout suits
going into the ladies' fitness center
at the small strip mall.
A goofy guy with a too-short
button up shirt, belly hanging out
and coke-bottle glasses walks out of
the video store next door holding a
black bag full of pornography and
god knows what else.
Another lady walks by headed to the gym,
with an ass the size of Texas and
he trips on the curb as he watches her
strut across the lot and enter the building.
He pushes his glasses back up off his nose
and gets into the car with the drooling dog.
I begin to see why they say
owners and animals look alike.

Thrift Store Surprise

He looked like a mean son of a bitch, ex-military; U.S. Marines,
at least that's what the sticker on his old Cadillac said.
He just sat in his car, window down, with his engine running,
chewing on the end of a fat cigar in the parking lot of
the Salvation Army thrift store in the shopping plaza.

I stood against the wall, breathing into my hands
trying to warm them from the desert cold, and

watching him pull on his stogie
left me unable to fight the urge to have a smoke, so
I fired up a menthol, it burned all the way down
mixed with the December air that felt like razor blades.

He shut off his car and rolled up his tinted windows,
and I watched as the car shook from side to side and
I wondered what the hell he could be doing in there.
The motions stopped and the door popped open and a
big, black boot touched the pavement, then
from behind the door, he stood up in view, he was
donning a bright red Santa Claus suit.

He turned his rear toward me and leaned into his car
as if to reach for something and then backed out holding
a cow bell in one hand and adjusting his Santa hat with the other.
He shut the door of his caddy and headed toward the entrance
of the thrift store. Half way through the parking lot,
he began to ring his bell and bellow out a merry
Ho! Ho! Ho! Merry Christmas!

Reality Check

She walked through Walmart with her cell phone to her ear.
The same kind of girl who has eighty-two mirror shots
of herself, in her bathroom, puckering her duck lips
on her Facebook wall that screams *look at me*, and
she's bitching about some whore named Lisa and how she's
going to *beat her fucking ass the next time she comes around.*
She was fired up, and didn't care who heard her;
moms with kids, preachers, and dressed up women
pushing empty buggies who go there after church
just so everyone can see them in their Sunday best
(of course that's why).
They could have bought their half gallon of milk
at the convenience store,
but then who would see them
because this reality TV generation tells us
you're nobody if nobody's looking.

An Old Man in the Park

He pulled a long, hard drag
from a loosely rolled cigarette
packed with cheap tobacco
mumbling something about shit
and how God damned it
while flashbacks of bombers
exploded in his mind.

Suburbia

There were rows and rows of them
lined up together, tucked between
sidewalks and square yards of
perfectly manicured grass.
And they all looked the same.
Same windows, same colors
same cars in the driveways,
boring four-door sedans
and little mini vans
with stick figure families
with dogs, holding hands
on the rear windshield.
Sleepy little suburbia.
Soccer moms—and
nine-to-five dads carrying
briefcases and flowers for
their depressed wives who
cook and clean and birth
spoiled children with
addictions to video games
and marijuana
stashed under their beds.
Sleepy little suburbia.
Home of pill-popping moms
masked with the thick makeup
of pretentious perfection
and locked away inside
cracker boxes—pretending
and playing house because

that's what girls are
supposed to do.

The Empty House Next Door

There's an empty house next door—
a brown-brick rancher they call it—
with a single wind chime
hanging on the front porch
just because no one has stolen it
yet.
It seems to say
leave me alone.
No curtains in the windows,
no kids playing in the yard,
no lights on at night,
no noises, no movement,
except when people stop by
to peek in the windows;
different cars, different people,
people with loud kids running around
and old people who wouldn't like
that I am a night owl
and play my music loud when I clean.
I hope no one moves in.

The Tin Man in a Pretty Yard

One day
all those things,
all those pretty, shiny things
will be nothing.
Nothing but tarnished trophies
of dust-covered dreams
in condemned castles, in houses
that never bore the feeling
There's no place like home,
and now instead, posts the sign

Estate Sale.

Things,
worth nothing more
than the rotted corpse who
sold his soul to acquire it.

Now,
those things
are purchased at a discount
by the strangers next door,
who embraced a minute,
and stopped
to smell the flowers,
the flowers his gardener tended.

Talk Radio

She came through the radio,
a soothing voice talking about
love and taking calls from listeners.

It's after midnight with Rosie.

A lady asks her;
When will I ever get over him?
Why does it have to hurt so bad?
And she's slinging and sucking snot
so loud it makes me want to puke.

The radio woman says to her,

At first you drive yourself mad
thinking about all the good things;
all the laughs, missing them, wanting them back,
and it hurts so bad, with a pain so sickening
you think it will never let go.

But then . . .
after awhile you start to remember
all the reasons it ended, all the tears
and all the bad things that hurt you
and it leaves you disgusted, and then,
that pain, it begins to dissipate
and you are finally free.

And before she could finish spewing her
cheesy words of wisdom that even
Hallmark writers wouldn't print,
I called bullshit;
nobody ever escapes.

John Brown

He likes the streets at night,
driving beneath the cavernous
sad, yellow glow of street lamps
and their faded halo rings
he thinks looks like angels
overlooking the dark,
watching crime unfold beneath them
in the dirty back alleys of the city,
but unable to stop it.

Useless—might as well be pitch black.
He thought of it like
the filth and grime beating out of the
smoked-out Cadillac in front of him, on
twenty inch spinning rims, littering
the silence with the sound of gunshots
and angry voices mad at the world.
A classic, with a trunk full of speakers—
dumb fucking kids.

Creeping past, he watches shadow-steppers
ducking back into the cut like ghosts
disappearing into the darkness,
and he knows they're up to no good.
They can hide, but they can't run—
they try.
But, after twenty years, he still drops them.

Fast talking woman on the radio
confirms his suspicions—*copy that*—
and he lights up the alley with red and blue,
and busts out his own noise that
they hate to hear as much as he hates
the garbage rolling out of their Cadillac,
and he's in pursuit.

The Lights Never Go Out

In the city where
the lights never go out
old man holds a cardboard sign
Vietnam Vet, please give
some people keep walking
some people don't
four hours and fifty bucks later
he hops a bus to the west side
meets with a runner
for a cutter
cuts his rock
and sucks his pipe
never hits like the first time
he says
in a motel room where
the lights never go out

Whiskey and Vinyl

In his hotel window,

he sat by candlelight
sipping whiskey
as he eased the needle down
cracking vinyl
washing her memory in
the best of Patsy Cline
because they were both
Crazy

Fools
chasing hearts too damn long
that didn't want to be caught
and he knew it
the first time he saw her
the way she flipped her head
in the other direction
like little Miss Too Good
but god was she pretty.

The Witness

One black eye and choke marks
around her tiny neck, she was crying
with a suitcase at her side, sitting on
a bus stop bench on the corner in the rain,
outside of a rundown hotel where
the flashing sign read *cheap hourly rates*
and he stood in the window, peeking from
behind the curtain, watching her
with disturbed eyes and what looked like
a smile on his grizzly, unshaven face.
The light turned green and she was still there.
In the rearview, the door opened, and she turned.
She haunted me the whole night; her eyes,
pained and empty. The morning paper headlines:
Man Found Shot in Local Hotel. No Suspect. No Witness.
I smiled.

Fucking Telemarketers

you know it's them
it's six o'clock in the morning
people with sense know better
you say hello
and it takes them a minute
then they go for it
all in without a breath
selling you shit
served up as a favor
and they'll give you ten days
to change your mind
and they'll pay you back
guaranteed
because it takes eleven
to find out
they were full of shit

Small Town Politician

there was a knock at the door
and there stood a mustache-covered smile
phony as imitation crab and
stunk like it too

his hand reached out to me
as he introduced himself
followed by a long spill about
how he's running for some
political seat in town and how he
sure would appreciate it if
I would vote for him on Tuesday

he said
I like to visit with the community
get to know them personally
and then something about
how he was a good friend of the lady
who lived here before
and how he could always count on her vote

how is she, he asked
she's dead, I replied

he looked at me and gave a
stunned and busted apology
then without permission
pushed a cardboard sign into my lawn

on Tuesday
I forgot his name

The Pneumonia

It was a doctor's office;
a small waiting lounge with
three rows of chairs stuck together.
If you weren't sick before you got there,
you sure as hell would be after you left,
carrying some contagious disease
from being forced to sit nearly
on someone's lap who was
spitting mucus when they hacked
and wiping snot on their hand.
She must have been his wife,
she was nagging like wives do.
"I bet you have the pneumonia,"
she kept saying, while he
continued to stare at his phone.
"I told you, you should have
let me bring you before it got bad,
but you never listen to me," she said.
And again, she repeated herself,
"I'm telling you, I bet you have the pneumonia."
His phone lit up and played some little tune.
"Who is that?" she said.
"It's Randall; he wants me to
go hunting with him in the morning."
That really twisted her panties up.
She got out of her chair, threw her arms up, and
as she was walking out the door
she began to yell at him,
"Oh my god. I can't believe you.
I can't believe you'd even consider

Candy From Strangers 57

going out in the freezing weather
to sit in the woods, after I have been
worried sick with you for three days!
Go! Go ahead if that's what you want to do,
but don't come home pissing and moaning to me
because you have the fucking pneumonia."

Early Risers

I pulled into the parking lot
taking up two spaces, waiting
till I finished my cigarette
before going inside.
It was early morning.
A street cleaner rode through,
circling and sweeping up
the littered lot.
Leaving it clean again for the
early risers.
A woman whipped in the space
in front of me and
walked in a fast stride
toward the door.
When she returned, she held a
clear grocery sack with a
bag of sugar inside.
I wondered why she would be
rushing out for sugar
at such an hour.
Was she baking?
Did she need it for coffee?
I don't know, but whatever the reason
she was in just as big a hurry
leaving as she was coming.
Whipping back out and
speeding off with her sugar.

Birds played and worked,
floating from lot to

rooftop of the strip mall.
Nests above windows of
empty spaces with lease signs.

A Sara Lee truck came.
The back door rose and
a man smoking a cigarette rolled a
crate of bread onto the platform
then lowered it down to the ground.
He stood there a minute,
hastily toking his smoke
before flipping it out into the lot
and wheeling the bread crate
toward the little grocery store.
Another fast stepper,
like the sugar lady,
both on a mission to get something done.
I was still in slow motion,
it was too damn early to be
moving that fast, I thought to myself
as I took another slow drag
from my cigarette
nearing the filter now.

Across the road
there was another lot
with three buildings:
a church, a funeral home,
and a florist.
I never noticed before,
but they go together.
Find God, die,
people buy you flowers

and you push them up.
It made me remember why I was
sitting in a parking lot
hazy eyed and people watching
at seven o'clock in the morning.
I was out of cigarettes.

The Girl at Register Three

she wanted to run
run far away from everyone who didn't get her
inside, she cried for a mother gone
not to death but to booze
and another man she
wanted her to call daddy
and she didn't understand that place
that house they called a home
when her father's wife came screaming
and no kind exchanges made
she only felt alone
and rejection was all she knew
but sixteen doesn't come with answers
she pondered as she rang up strangers
buying milk in her checkout lane
smiling through pain and counting back change
the bag boy flirts and she wonders if
he would go with her
and she daydreams of stealing the drawer
then running and living in danger
at least then
she might feel something in her veins
something hot coursing through
to melt the frigid hate
and she would feel alive
even if the only ones trying to find her
were the cops and maybe Jesus

Finding Jesus at the Discount Grocery

her nails were painted hot pink
distracting and curious for a woman her age
with graying hair salted in between her darkening roots
and I watched them as she cracked open a roll of quarters
and never looking up, she says, with a high pitched voice
and a lazy southern drawl, the kind where the words
seem to all run together,
hower-ya-doin-t'day
kindly, I reply with *fine, thank you,* and then
three words I wish I had never uttered
how. are. you.
those three words set a trap I thought I'd never escape
and it all started with an *oh honey, let me tell ya*

there was a crazy ex-husband, a whore of a sister,
and a pregnant daughter who was only fifteen
a car with a blown motor, an eviction notice,
but she'd met the man of her dreams
(it was indeed, a country song if I'd ever heard one)

she continued filling me in on all the days of her life,
slowly bagging the last of my groceries and I . . .
I was anxiously awaiting a pause so that I might interrupt,
but it was like being on the phone with your mother
where you say goodbye a dozen times but they have to tell you
just one more thing . . .
and just as I dangled from the edge of sheer rudeness
ready to lose my grip, it stopped
sighing, she exhaled a breath like she had been drowning,
and took just a second to smack her gum she had tried to

keep tucked in her jaw, but kept peeking out at me
and then she said,
*ahhh well, it'll all work out though, I found Jesus
you-hava-goodun-okay*

Truck Stop Bathroom

There were sniffling sobs
bouncing off the grungy walls
of the truck-stop bathroom
off highway seventy-five south.
I ripped a paper towel from the
dispenser beside the sinks
and used it to open the stall.
Shit.
Someone forgot to flush.
This is the women's room, right?
I backed out, my hand cupped
around my nose and mouth
as I moved down two doors.
That's as clean as it'll get,
I thought.
Then I placed toilet paper
over the dingy yellow seat
and eased down slowly
so it wouldn't slip off.
The sobs and sniffles continued.
I thought about asking,
but I didn't.
I finished, flushed, and
went for the soap.
I left the water running
while I scrubbed like a
doctor preparing for surgery,
and when I turned it off
she was standing behind me
in the doorway of her stall.

She stared at me like
she wanted to ask something,
but she didn't.
I gave her a tight-lipped grin
and walked out.
But I always wondered,
what was her story . . .

Thank you for reading *Candy From Strangers*. Now it's your turn to tell me a story. Use this as your writing prompt, then visit my website, http://kellieelmore.com/whats-her-story/

Use the password: strangerstory

and tell me . . . what was her story?

About the Author

Kellie Elmore is a writer who believes self-expression is most beautiful in its pure, raw and unedited form, transforming the simplest words into something you can feel. Kellie finds inspiration in nature and in the humble surroundings of her "backyard" – Southeast Tennessee. Through her charming prose and engrossing narratives, Kellie writes freely on many subjects both fiction and semi-autobiographical, penning her way through cherished and magical moments as well as tragic losses. Her goal is to take readers back, rekindle a memory, or elicit a feeling.

www.ingramcontent.com/pod-product-compliance
Lightning Source LLC
Chambersburg PA
CBHW070759050426
42452CB00012B/2406